My World

Baby Animals

by Tammy J. Schlepp

Copper Beech Books
Brookfield, Connecticut

Contents

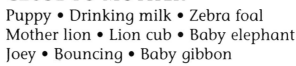

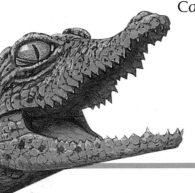

© Aladdin Books Ltd 2000

Designed and produced by
Aladdin Books Ltd
28 Percy Street
London W1P 0LD

First published in
the United States in 2000 by
Copper Beech Books,
an imprint of
The Millbrook Press
2 Old New Milford Road
Brookfield, Connecticut 06804

ISBN 0-7613-1218-8

Cataloging-in-Publication data is on
file at the Library of Congress

Printed in U.A.E.

All rights reserved

Coordinator
Jim Pipe

Design
Flick Book Design and Graphics

Picture Research
Brian Hunter Smart

Come one! Come all!

Meet the baby animals!

Some are born alive. Some hatch from eggs.

Some look like their parents.

Some change as they grow.

Turn the page and you'll see!

Baboons

Hi, I'm a little puppy.

Do you know what I do?

Puppy

I love to play. I love to cuddle.

If I get hungry, I drink my mother's milk.

Furry feet and wagging tail.
That's how you know I'm not a snail.

Drinking
milk

Hello, I'm a zebra foal.

That's a baby zebra.

Do you know
what I do?
I gallop with
my mother.

Zebra foal

Mane, hoof, and striped hairy tail.

Zebras have these, but not a whale.

Howdy, I'm a baby lion.

You can call me lion cub.

Do you know what I do?

I ride in my mother's mouth to a new home.

Fur, whiskers, teeth, and claws.

Lion cubs have these—and paws.

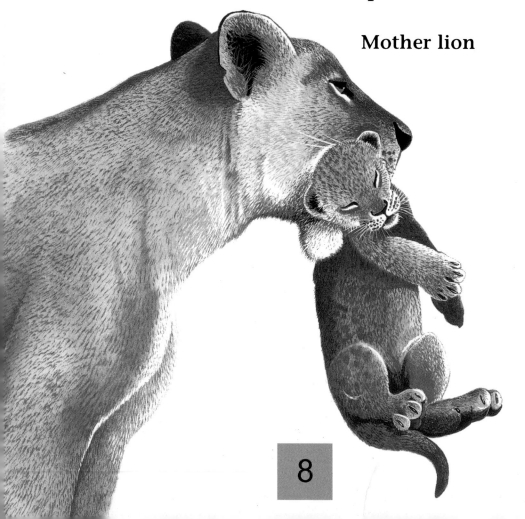

Mother lion

A lion cub
Can you see its paws?

Hello, I'm a baby elephant.

Do you know what I do?

I eat with my trunk.

That's my very long nose.

Baby elephant

Wrinkles, trunk, and very thick skin.

Baby elephants have these.

So do their kin.

A joey

Can you see its body?

Hi, I'm a baby kangaroo. You can call
me joey. Do you know what I do?
I ride inside my mother's pouch.

Bouncing

Strong tail, long ears, and huge feet.
Joeys have these. Don't you think that's neat?

Howdy, I'm a baby gibbon.

I swing through a tree

with my mom.

I'm a frisky child.

Hey, Mom, watch me!

A baby gibbon hangs on tight.

Hi, I'm a baby duckling.

Do you know what I do?

Duckling

I grow inside an egg
and I paddle in the water.

Egg breaks

I quack a lot and I have
webbed feet to let you
know I'm not a parakeet.

Swimming ducklings

Hello, I'm a baby penguin.

My name is chick and I hatch from an egg.

Chick

Penguins

18

Do you know what I do?

I waddle on the ice.

I swim swiftly in the water.

Webbed feet and brown feathers.

I don't mind cold weather.

Howdy, I'm a baby crocodile.

Do you know what I do?

Baby crocodiles

20

Crocodile mother

I hatch from an egg.

I swim in water.

Sharp, pointy teeth and swinging tail, too.

Get close to me and I might bite you!

Hello, I'm a tadpole.

Do you know what I do?

Frogs' eggs

I hatch from an egg and swim like a fish in water.

Tadpole

When I grow up—SURPRISE!

I'll be a frog with

bulging eyes

and a taste for flies.

**Growing
legs**

Sorry, I don't eat french fries!

Frog

23

Baby spiders
How many legs do
they have?

Hi, I'm a baby spider. I came from an egg.

I have lots and lots of sisters and brothers!

Howdy, I'm a caterpillar.

I came from an egg.
Do you know what I do?

Egg

Caterpillar

I eat and eat and grow and grow!

Shell

Then I wrap myself in a hard shell.
When I come out, what a change!

I used to crawl but now I'll fly.
You see I'll be a butterfly!

Butterfly

27

Can You Find?

Some baby animals have fur.
Others have smooth bodies.

Can you find which baby animal
has each skin?

A

B

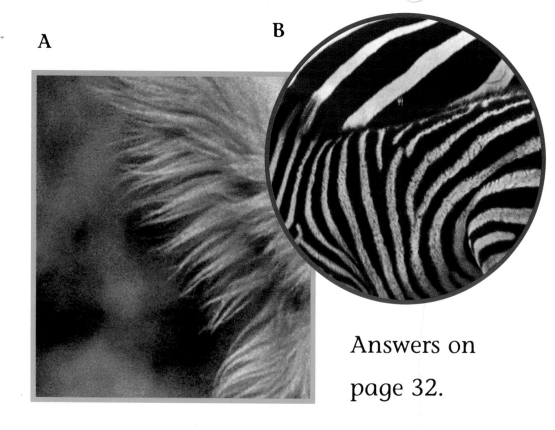

Answers on
page 32.

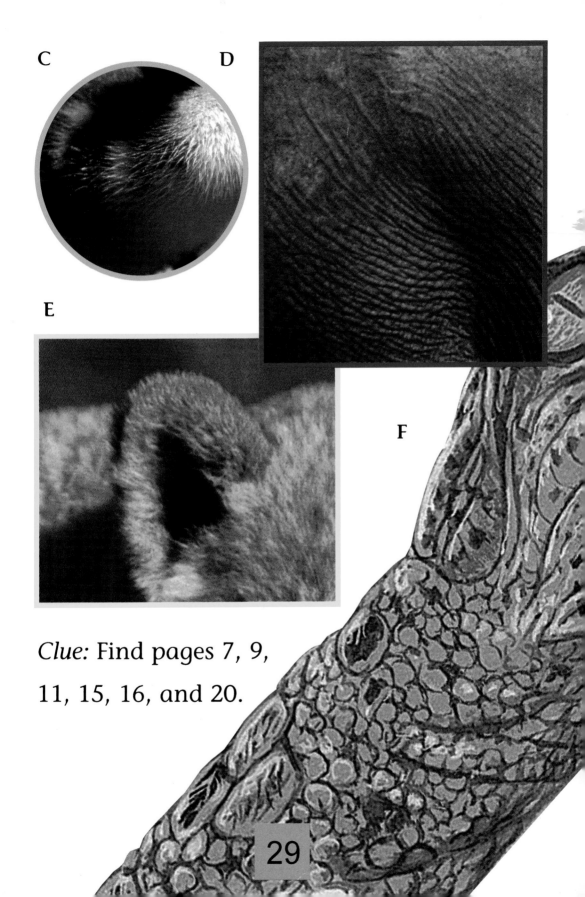

C

D

E

F

Clue: Find pages 7, 9, 11, 15, 16, and 20.

Do You Know?

Do you know these animals? Can you guess which of them lay eggs?

Parakeet

Snake

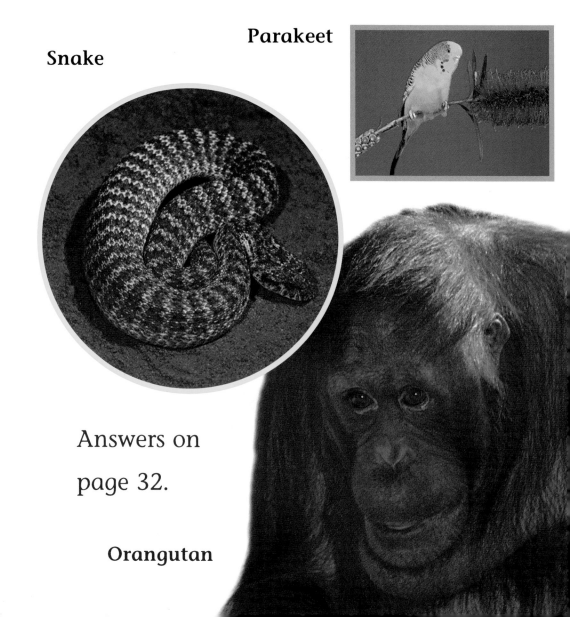

Answers on page 32.

Orangutan

Dolphin

Hen

Grasshopper

Frog

Index

ANSWERS TO QUESTIONS

Pages 28-29 – **A** shows a gibbon's fur • **B** shows a zebra's coat • **C** shows a duckling's soft feathers • **D** shows the skin of an elephant • **E** shows a lion cub's fur • **F** shows a crocodile's scaly skin.

Pages 30-31 – **Snakes** are reptiles and lay eggs like a crocodile • **Parakeets** and **hens** are birds and lay eggs like a duck • **Orangutans** and **dolphins** don't lay eggs. They have babies like a dog • A **grasshopper** has eggs like a butterfly • A **frog** lays eggs.

Photocredits: Abbreviations: t-top, m-middle, b-bottom, r-right, l-left, c-center.
Cover, 2tl, 2ml, 6-7, 10-11, 18c, 18-19, 23, 28mr, 29tr, 30 all, 31t, 31ml, 31br—Digital Stock. 1, 17, 31mr—J.Foxx Images. 3, 9, 29ml—Corbis. 2mr, 26mr—S.Moody/Dembinsky/FLPA-Images of Nature. 4—Select Pictures. 12—D.Hosking/FLPA-Images of Nature. 14-15, 28bl—Gerard Lacz/FLPA-Images of Nature. 16, 29tl—Stockbyte. 21—Brake/Sunset/FLPA-Images of Nature. 22t—W.Meinderts/Foto Natura/FLPA-Images of Nature. 22b—A.J.Roberts/FLPA-Images of Nature. 24-25—Silvestris Fotoservice/FLPA-Images of Nature. 26ml, 27b—L.West/FLPA-Images of Nature. 27tl—Treat Dividson/FLPA-Images of Nature.
Illustrator: Chris Shields—Wildlife Art Ltd.